NATIONAL GEOGRAPHIC

T0045531

Places to Visit

Nick Bruce

There are many famous places to visit in the United States.

Have you been to the **Grand Canyon**? It is in Arizona.

The **Grand Canyon** is a deep valley with steep sides. In some places it is 18 miles wide. Other places are less than one mile wide.

Have you been to **Yellowstone National Park**? It is in Wyoming, Idaho, and Montana.

Yellowstone is the oldest National Park in the world. It is one of the largest safe areas for wildlife in the United States.

Have you been to
Niagara Falls?
It is in New York.

Niagara Falls is the largest waterfall in North America. It is made up of two waterfalls, the Horseshoe Falls and the American Falls.

Have you been to
Mount St. Helens?
It is in Washington.

Mount St. Helens is a volcano. It erupted in 1980 forming a crater on top.

Have you been to
Mammoth Cave?
It is in Kentucky.

Mammoth Cave is a huge underground cave. There are stalactites and underground lakes in the cave.

Have you been to the **Everglades**? It is in Florida.

The **Everglades** is a huge marsh. It is known as a river of grass.

Have you been to these famous places?

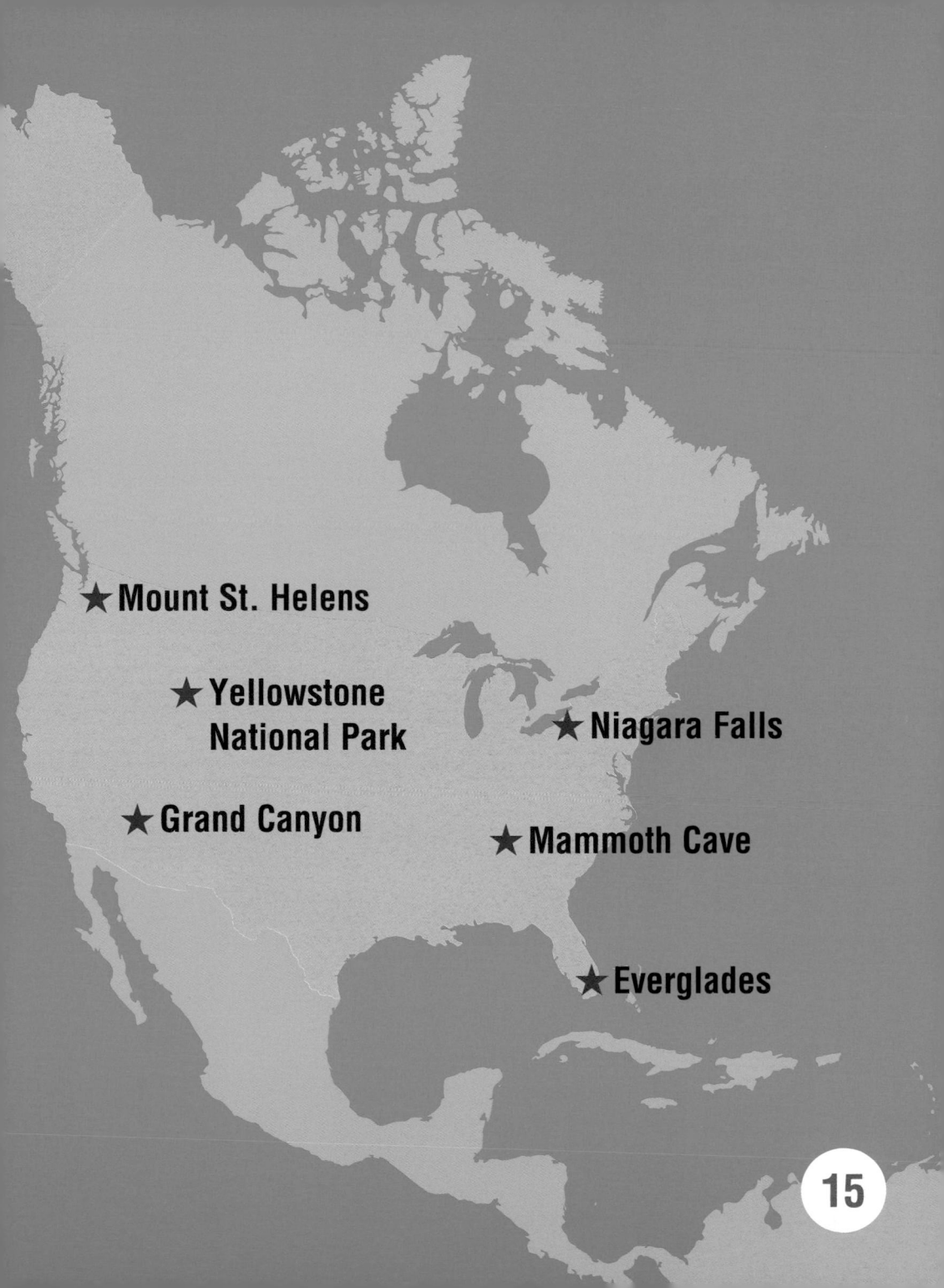
Mount St. Helens
Yellowstone National Park
Niagara Falls
Grand Canyon
Mammoth Cave
Everglades

Index

Arizona	2
Everglades	12–13, 15
Florida	12
Grand Canyon	2–3, 15
Idaho	4
Kentucky	10
Mammoth Cave	10–11, 15
Montana	4
Mount St. Helens	8–9, 15
New York	6
Niagara Falls	6–7, 15
Washington	8
Wyoming	4
Yellowstone National Park	4–5, 15